JAMES BOND

THE ULTIMATE QUIZ BOOK

UNOFFICIAL & UNAUTHORISED

ACORN BOOKS

Chris McAuley
& Jack Goldstein

James Bond – The Ultimate Quiz Book
Published in 2020 by
Acorn Books
www.acornbooks.co.uk

Acorn Books is an imprint of
Andrews UK Limited
www.andrewsuk.com

"Do you expect me to talk?"

"No, Mr. Bond. I expect you to die!"
—*Goldfinger*

CONTENTS

INTRODUCTION

The world of James Bond is rich and detailed with twenty-five films released as part of the Eon franchise and two more that cause huge debate among fans as to whether they are 'canon'. Bond himself has changed over the years; not only in terms of the actor playing him, but also the way he fits into our modern world... and even – dare we say it – his code of ethics. His 'girls' have evolved too – from helpless beauties picking up sea shells to field agents just as ruthless as the man himself; the story of Bond is as much a story about our society as it is the world of spying and intrigue.

This book contains five hundred questions (and answers) to test your knowledge of the first sixty years of Bond. Whether it's the villains, the henchmen, the gadgets, girls or guns, your knowledge of the entire Bond universe will be put to use.

We are, of course, grateful to Ian Fleming, Eon productions, the Broccolis, the actors who have played Bond and his friends, and everyone else involved in bringing the world of the super-spy to life. We've thoroughly enjoyed the last sixty years... so here's to sixty more!

Good luck in the quiz!

Chris McAuley & Jack Goldstein
March 2021

THE QUESTIONS

DR. NO

1. In which way does Dr. No die?

2. What organization does Felix Leiter work for?

3. What is the name of the island that Dr. No uses as his headquarters?

4. What is Honey Ryder collecting when Bond first encounters her?

5. What does Bond discover about the rocks that Strangeways is in possession of?

6. Which actress played the role of Honey Ryder?

7. What is the distinguishing physical characteristic of Dr. No?

8. What does Dent leave in Bond's hotel, hoping to kill him?

9. Which newspaper does the photographer claim to work for?

10. What type of gun is Bond given to complete his assignment?

Turn to page 54 for the answers

11. One of the most iconic moments in Bond history is when Auric Goldfinger has captured 007, and we see that Bond is trapped on a table. By what type of cutting tool is he about to be eviscerated?

12. In *Live and Let Die* Bond is captured by heroin kingpin and diplomat Dr. Kananga who leaves him on a small rock in the middle of a pond. Which aquatic predators are about to eat him?

13. In *The Man with the Golden Gun*, inside which type of amusement park ride does Scaramanga attempt to kill Bond?

14. Which method do assassins Mr. Wint and Mr. Kidd use in an attempt to eliminate Bond in *Diamonds are Forever*?

15. It seems like every time Bond tries to sleep, someone is trying to kill him. There's no better example of this than in *You Only Live Twice*. Which method was used to try and put Bond to sleep for good?

16. What vehicular peril did Roger Moore's Bond narrowly escape in *A View to a Kill*?

17. In *Tomorrow Never Dies*, which obscure torture style does Dr. Kaufman use on 007?

18. Which part of Jaws's body was replaced by razor sharp metal?

19. In the 21st century version of *Casino Royale*, 007's drinking habits almost kill him as a result of which near-fatal condition?

20. Famke Janssen plays the sadistic ex-soviet pilot Xenia Onatopp. How does she attempt to crush James Bond?

Turn to page 55 for the answers

21. At the beginning of the film, what game is being played by the two men in Venice?

22. Which item does Spectre wish to steal from the Russians?

23. What is Rosa Klebb's code number in SPECTRE?

24. What does Bond write on Tatiana's photograph?

25. What does Ali Kerim Bey use to spy on the Russian Consulate?

26. Which special gadget does Q give to Bond to help with his mission?

27. When Bond reaches the Russian consulate, what does he ask the man at the desk, twice?

28. When Grant first meets Bond, what name does he give?

29. What does Bond throw into the water at the end of the film?

30. How does Bond kill Grant?

Turn to page 56 for the answers

FILM YEARS - PART 1

In which year were each of the following Bond films first released?

31. *Dr. No*

32. *Spectre*

33. *Live and Let Die*

34. *For Your Eyes Only*

35. *GoldenEye*

36. *Thunderball*

37. *The World Is Not Enough*

38. *Die Another Day*

39. *Diamonds Are Forever*

40. *Moonraker*

Turn to page 57 for the answers

41. The Bank of England gives Bond a gold bar; how much is he told it is worth?

42. What model of car does Q provide 007 with?

43. What happens when Bond presses the red button on the car's gearstick?

44. How does Goldfinger cheat at cards?

45. How does Bond win his golf game with Goldfinger?

46. When Bond wakes up on the plane, whom does he meet?

47. To which city does Bond go when tracking Goldfinger?

48. What is the name of the nerve gas that Goldfinger plans to use?

49. Which characters make up his car license plate?

50. How does Goldfinger die?

Turn to page 58 for the answers

GADGETS & GUNS

51. In *From Russia With Love*, what type of weapon does Red Grant have concealed in his wristwatch?

52. In the opening sequence of *Goldfinger*, what does Bond use to conceal his presence when swimming underwater to a Mexican drugs complex?

53. In *Diamonds are Forever*, what does Bond use to convince Tiffany Case of his assumed identity?

54. In *The World Is Not Enough*, what does Bond use to tell him how many people are armed when he enters the casino?

55. In *You Only Live Twice*, what does Helga Brandt use to disorientate Bond while she parachutes from the plane, leaving him on a crash course?

56. What unusual item does Bond ask Q to provide him in order to pose as Scaramanga in *The Man with the Golden Gun*?

57. In which piece of Bond's equipment is a gun hidden during the downhill ski chase in *The Spy Who Loved Me*?

58. In *Thunderball*, which gadget allows Bond to escape from Largo's shark pool?

59. In *Moonraker*, what does Bond use to shoot Drax before launching him into space?

60. At the beginning of *Tomorrow Never Dies*, what gadget does Bond use to start the confusion at the arms bazaar?

Turn to page 59 for the answers

61. How does Bond escape from the roof?

62. Who does SPECTRE plan to demand a ransom from?

63. What is the fighter jet carrying that the SPECTRE agents steal?

64. Which creature is featured in the logo of SPECTRE?

65. Where does Bond hide a tape recorder in his hotel room?

66. What is the name of Largo's boat?

67. How does Bond kill Vargas?

68. What colour is Bond's wetsuit?

69. In what sport do Largo and Bond partake?

70. How many 00 agents are there in the room with M and the Home Secretary?

Turn to page 60 for the answers

THEME TUNES - PART 1

Who sang the following theme tunes?

71. *Tomorrow Never Dies*

72. *Die Another Day*

73. *From Russia with Love*

74. *GoldenEye*

75. *A View to a Kill*

76. *Licence to Kill*

77. *You Only Live Twice*

78. *The Living Daylights*

79. *Skyfall*

80. *Thunderball*

Turn to page 61 for the answers

YOU ONLY LIVE TWICE

81. At the beginning of the film, what happens to the USA's spacecraft?

82. Which famous children's author actually wrote the screenplay for the film?

83. What is the password that Miss Moneypenny provides Bond with in order to make contact with the SIS?

84. How does Henderson die?

85. What is Tanaka's first name?

86. What does Bond say after Hans falls into the piranha pool?

87. How does Aki die?

88. When does Blofeld spot Bond after he poses as an astronaut?

89. What is the name of the helicopter that Bond asks Q to bring to Japan?

90. What happens to Bond's dinghy at the end of the film?

Turn to page 62 for the answers

91. In *Dr. No*, Anthony Dawson plays which crooked scientist?

92. In *From Russia With Love*, Robert Shaw plays one of the most dangerous henchmen in the series. When he is recruited, how does Rosa Klebb test his strength?

93. In *Goldfinger*, how does Oddjob die?

94. Name the beautiful female assassin in *Thunderball*.

95. Karin Dor plays a femme fatale in *You Only Live Twice*. But what is her SPECTRE number?

96. In *On Her Majesty's Secret Service*, which character does Ilse Steppat play?

97. In *Diamonds Are Forever*, Bond is harassed by a pair of assassins called Mr. Wint and Mr. Kidd. How do they die?

98. In *Live And Let Die*, Dr. Kananga has a huge henchman called Tee Hee. What part of Tee Hee is missing?

99. To the nearest inch, how tall was Hervé Villechaize, who plays Nick Nack in *The Man with the Golden Gun*?

100. Which actor plays Jaws in the Bond series?

Turn to page 63 for the answers

101. Which card game does Bond play at the hotel's casino?

102. What does Bond ask Draco for in return for marrying his daughter?

103. When we first see 007, what is the first line he speaks?

104. What sporting event are Draco and Bond watching when first introduced to each other?

105. Which winter sport do the women show Bond how to play?

106. What is written on Bond's leg in lipstick?

107. What is the nickname of the twelve young women in the Swiss Alps clinic?

108. At the clinic, what item of menswear is Bond noticeably wearing?

109. Name the European city Bond travels to when investigating the lawyer?

110. What is the Bond family motto revealed as?

Turn to page 64 for the answers

QUOTES - PART 1

In which Bond film will you hear the following quotes?

111. I think he got the point.

112. I thought Christmas only comes once a year.

113. Are you looking for shells too?

114. Now there's a name to die for.

115. Ejector seat? You must be joking!

116. I admit killing you would be a pleasure.

117. One of us smells like a tart's handkerchief.

118. What did you expect, an exploding pen? We don't really go for that anymore.

119. Go backwards forwards quickly!

120. Don't touch that... that's my lunch!

Turn to page 65 for the answers

121. How does Blofeld die at the start of the film?

122. How does Mr. Wint kill the dentist?

123. What vehicle does Bond use to travel to Amsterdam?

124. Where do 80% of the world's diamonds come from, according to Sir Donald?

125. How does Tiffany Case check Bond's identity?

126. What game does Bond play in the casino when he meets Plenty O'Toole?

127. What unusual vehicle does Bond use to escape from W Techtronics?

128. How does Bond kill Peter Franks?

129. What is the name of the show playing at the Whyte House Hotel?

130. Who masquerades as a customs officer when Bond arrives in Los Angeles?

Turn to page 66 for the answers

ANAGRAMS - VILLAINS & HENCHMEN

Here are some anagrams of well-known Bond villains or henchmen... but which ones?

131. Minor Zax

132. Cliff Here

133. Whet Rim

134. Had Ox Rug

135. Ricks Vat Zoo

136. Visual Oral

137. Pope Anatoxin

138. A Nag Drank

139. Clever Tailor

140. Soya Splurge

Turn to page 67 for the answers

141. How many British agents are killed before the opening credits?

142. What is the secondary feature of the watch that Q gives to Bond?

143. Of which island is Dr. Kananga the Prime Minister?

144. What is the name of the chain of restaurants owned by Kananga?

145. Which tarot card does Bond pick in his first encounter with Solitaire?

146. What does Tee Hee do with Bond's gun?

147. What is the name of Dr. Kananga's alternative identity?

148. What vehicle does Bond use to escape when being chased by the police?

149. What does Rosie Carver (allegedly) find on her pillow?

150. How does Bond kill the snake in his hotel suite?

Turn to page 68 for the answers

FILM YEARS - PART 2

Which Bond film was released in each of the following years?

151. 1989

152. 1969

153. 1983

154. 1985

155. 1977

156. 1974

157. 1964

158. 2008

159. 1987

160. 1997

Turn to page 69 for the answers

161. Which actor – famous for his portrayal of Dracula – starred in the role of Francisco Scaramanga?

162. Where does Scaramanga find his gun in the opening sequence?

163. …and during that sequence, which 00 agent did Scaramanga kill?

164. What is etched on the golden bullet that Bond receives?

165. How much does Scaramanga charge per hit?

166. What is the name of the club that Bond visits in order to find Scaramanga?

167. What is the name of the Wrecked ship that MI6 uses as its headquarters in Hong Kong?

168. What is Scaramanga's physical abnormality?

169. What is the name of the bullet maker that Bond meets?

170. Where does the belly dancer keep the bullet that killed Bond's colleague?

Turn to page 70 for the answers

BOND GIRLS

Which actress played each of the following roles?

171. Honey Ryder?

172. Pussy Galore?

173. Mrs. Bond?

174. Tiffany Case?

175. Jinx?

176. Solitaire?

177. Mary Goodnight?

178. Octopussy?

179. Strawberry Fields?

180. May Day?

Turn to page 71 for the answers

181. What is the codename of Major Amasova?

182. What patriotic pattern is on Bond's parachute?

183. What distinctive feature does Jaws have?

184. What does Anya use to knock out Bond on the boat?

185. What item does Kalba attempt to sell to Bond?

186. What does Q use to decapitate a dummy?

187. What type of car does Q deliver to Bond?

188. Bond assumes the identity of Roger Sterling. What was his profession?

189. Which Italian island is featured in the film?

190. What souvenir does Bond buy in Austria?

Turn to page 72 for the answers

A GROSS AMOUNT OF MONEY

Here are the top ten grossing Bond films as of March 2021... but they're in the wrong order. Can you list them in the correct order, from highest to lowest?

191. *Goldeneye*

192. *Casino Royale*

193. *Spectre*

194. *Skyfall*

195. *Moonraker*

196. *Octopussy*

197. *Die Another Day*

198. *The World Is Not Enough*

199. *Tomorrow Never Dies*

200. *Quantum of Solace*

Turn to page 73 for the answers

201. Who throws Bond out of a plane at the start of the film?

202. What gadget does Q give Bond during their meeting with M?

203. Where does Bond find the hidden safe in Drax's mansion?

204. How does Corinne Dufour die?

205. Bond travels to Venice to investigate a manufacturer of which type of material?

206. Which organization does Goodhead work for?

207. What happens to the steel cable when Bond is atop the cable car?

208. What do the men who capture Bond and Goodhead pose as?

209. What does Goodhead's perfume bottle double as?

210. What does Chang land on when he is thrown through the clock tower window?

Turn to page 74 for the answers

211. Which actor was 58 years old when his final Bond film was released?

212. Who played James Bond in the most films?

213. Which actor played Bond just twice?

214. Which actor starred as 007 in a total of four films, spanning the turn of the millennium?

215. Gold is a recurring theme in the Bond series. But which gold-related Bond film featured Christopher Lee?

216. Starring Sean Connery as Agent 007, what was the first official Bond movie ever released?

217. Which group performed the title song for *The Living Daylights?*

218. What has become known as 007's preferred cocktail?

219. George Lazenby only played Bond on film once. What was the name of the film?

220. Who played Bond in the *original* film version of *Casino Royale*, released in 1968?

Turn to page 75 for the answers

221. Whose grave does Bond lay flowers on at the start of the film?

222. Who takes control of Bond's helicopter?

223. …and what does he offer Bond to let him go?

224. The *St. Georges* is equipped with a device called an ATAC. What does ATAC stand for?

225. What does the crew of the St. Georges accidently capture, leading to their deaths?

226. What message appears in Bond's hotel bathroom when he runs the hot tap?

227. What is Milos Columbo known as in the Greek Underworld, according to Kristatos?

228. What item is Luigi holding in his hand when Bond finds him dead?

229. How does the countess Lisl von Schlaf die?

230. How are the three men who attack Bond at the rink dressed?

Turn to page 76 for the answers

LYRICS - EASY

What comes next after these Bond theme lyrics?

231. Golden words he will pour in your ear, but his lies can't…

232. Any woman he wants, he'll get; he will…

233. Hold one up and then caress it; touch it…

234. The coldest blood runs through my veins…

235. I wasn't lookin', but…

236. You'll never know how I watched you…

237. You only live twice, or so it seems…

238. From Russia with love, I fly to you. Much wiser since my…

239. Sigmund Freud…

240. Face to face in secret places…

Turn to page 77 for the answers

241. How does Bond disguise his face when infiltrating the base in Cuba?

242. What type of vehicle does he use when escaping the military base?

243. Which 00 agent dies while delivering a fake Fabergé egg?

244. What is the name of the egg that is up for auction?

245. At which game does Bond beat Kamal Khan?

246. How does Bond track the fake egg?

247. While searching Octopussy's room, Bond discovers a leaflet for which event?

248. Where does General Orlov plan on detonating a nuclear bomb?

249. What is unusual about the vehicle Bond uses to pursue the train carrying the bomb?

250. What 'sporting' weapon does Vijay use during the car chase?

Turn to page 78 for the answers

251. What is Francisco Scaramanga's legendary weapon known as?

252. Why is Bond told to abandon his mission at the start of *Tomorrow Never Dies*?

253. True or false: there have been more Bond films featuring an Aston Martin than those without?

254. How many actors have portrayed James Bond in official movies?

255. Name any one of the three musicians to have recorded an alternative opening song for *Thunderball*?

256. How many Bond movies had Daniel Craig filmed by the end of 2020?

257. Who plays 006 in *GoldenEye*?

258. In how many movies did Sean Connery play James Bond?

259. True or false: the theme song for *Skyfall* reached number one in the UK and the USA?

260. Which agent is played by Denise Richards?

Turn to page 79 for the answers

261. At the start of the film, in what shaped necklace is the microchip hidden?

262. Which actor plays the role of Max Zorin?

263. What is the name of Zorin's horse?

264. After killing Aubergine, off what famous landmark does May Day parachute?

265. When staying at Zorin's estate, where does Bond find a listening device hidden?

266. Where is Tibbett when he is killed by May Day?

267. How does Zorin attempt to kill Bond and Stacey when they are in the elevator?

268. Which region in America does Zorin plan on destroying by causing a double Earthquake?

269. Who dies while transporting a bomb from the mineshaft into open ground?

270. Which famous landmark does Zorin's blimp crash into?

Turn to page 80 for the answers

ANAGRAMS - FILM TITLES

Can you unscramble these anagrams? They are all titles of Bond films...

271. Cosy Spout

272. Dateline Devil

273. Ginger Fold

274. Evil Koala Wit

275. A Lacy Erosion

276. Ear or Monk

277. Halt Blunder

278. Needy Ogle

279. Tickle el Colin

280. Respect

Turn to page 81 for the answers

281. In which British overseas territory does Bond land at the beginning of the film?

282. How does Bond smuggle General Koskov out of Czechoslovakia?

283. What does Q call his rocket launcher that is hidden inside a cassette tape player?

284. What does *Smiert Spionam* mean?

285. What does Necros disguise himself as in order to infiltrate the MI6 safe house?

286. What song does 007 have to whistle to activate the stun gas in his keyring?

287. Which actor plays General Pushkin?

288. What fake name is shown on Bond's passport at the Moroccan border?

289. After Bond's Aston Martin self-destructs, what unusual (even for him) method of transport does he use to escape from the KGB?

290. What type of container is used to hide the diamonds?

Turn to page 82 for the answers

291. In which film does 007 not drive a car throughout the whole movie?

292. In how many films does Jaws appear?

293. Which cocktail is Bond's go-to across the series?

294. What is unusual about his choice?

295. Who is the ultimate leader of SPECTRE?

296. What nationality is Xenia Onatopp?

297. What supernatural power does Solitaire supposedly possess?

298. What is Bond's watch brand of choice in the Pierce Brosnan era?

299. Which Bond film is the shortest in length?

300. How many people have portrayed M over the course of the Eon films?

Turn to page 83 for the answers

301. How does Bond capture Sanchez at the beginning of the film?

302. How do 007 and Felix Leiter arrive at the latter's wedding?

303. How does Sanchez attempt to kill Felix?

304. What does Bond disguise himself as in order to access Krest's boat?

305. What was the name of Bond's friend who is killed by Krest's men?

306. When 007 is driving the tanker, how does he avoid a rocket that is fired at him?

307. In what liquid does Sanchez's men dissolve the cocaine, in order to make it untraceable?

308. What animal does Sanchez keep as a pet?

309. Which fictional country does Bond travel to in order to stop Sanchez?

310. Q gives Bond some plastic explosive hidden inside which household item?

Turn to page 84 for the answers

THEME TUNES - PART 2

Name the theme song performed by the following artistes...

311. Louis Armstrong

312. Rita Coolidge

313. Sheena Easton

314. Sam Smith

315. Chris Cornell

316. Lulu

317. Byron Lee and the Dragonaires

318. Paul McCartney & Wings

319. Carly Simon

320. Jack White & Alicia Keys

Turn to page 85 for the answers

321. How does Bond access the Russian chemical facility at the start of the movie?

322. Which actor plays 006?

323. What is the name of the yacht where the Canadian admiral is killed?

324. What type of helicopter does Xenia Onatopp steal?

325. What happens when the GoldenEye satellite is fired?

326. What name does 006 use as a codename in order to conceal his identity?

327. Where is the huge satellite that 006 uses as his base hidden?

328. What song is Irina signing when Valentin tells her to 'take a hike'?

329. What happens to the man who uses the phone box as 007 and Q are talking?

330. How long are the timers set by 006 for the bomb on the train?

Turn to page 86 for the answers

331. Who is in the car with Bond when using a 2CV as an escape vehicle?

332. What was the name of Roger Moore's autobiography?

333. What was the last film in which Moore played Bond?

334. To whom is Bond speaking when he utters the line "I am now aiming precisely at your groin. So speak or forever hold your piece."

335. In what car did Bond make a corkscrew jump over a river?

336. True or false: the stunt made use of computer modelling to calculate the various parameters?

337. *The Man with the Golden Gun* has the lowest kill count of any Bond film. Throughout the course of the film, how many people does Roger Moore send to meet their maker?

338. Incredibly, Roger Moore suffers from hoplophobia. What is this condition?

339. In what year was Sir Roger Moore knighted by the Queen?

340. True or false: it was Roger Moore who uttered this classic line: "Keeping the British end up, Sir"?

Turn to page 87 for the answers

341. What device does Gupta obtain at the Arms Bazaar?

342. What quip does Bond utter after he activates the ejector seat?

343. Which actor plays the role of Elliot Carver?

344. What is the headline Carver writes after *H.M.S. Devonshire* is destroyed?

345. Which language is Bond brushing up on when Moneypenny calls him?

346. How is Q dressed when he meets Bond at Hamburg airport?

347. What is the name of the assassin who kills Paris Carver and threatens Bond?

348. What do Bond and Wai Lin use to descend from the top floor of Carver's building?

349. What is the name of the newspaper that Carver owns?

350. How does Bond steer his remote-control car?

Turn to page 88 for the answers

HARDER ANAGRAMS - FILM TITLES

Here are some more Bond movie titles for you to unscramble – though these are a little harder than before…

351. Stealth Dinghy Vigil

352. Savvy Arena Engineer

353. You Looney Fryers

354. Yellow Voice Unity

355. Defensive Radar Room

356. Rotten Household Wing

357. Worn Morris Devotee

358. Warmish Soviet Flour

359. Ride Honey Data

360. Empty Whoosh Delve

Turn to page 89 for the answers

361. Where is the trigger for the stun gas that Bond releases when meeting the banker?

362. What does 007 say to Moneypenny after she throws the cigar in the bin?

363. On which landmark does Bond land after falling from a hot air balloon?

364. When Elektra King is kidnapped, how much is the ransom demand?

365. Who shot the bullet into Renard's brain?

366. …and what does the bullet prevent him from being able to do?

367. What Q-branch device does Bond use at the casino to see who is carrying a weapon?

368. True or false: Christmas Jones is a medical doctor?

369. Which card game does Elektra play with Zukovsky?

370. How does Bond save Elektra after they are caught in a small avalanche?

Turn to page 90 for the answers

371. How many official James Bond Films have been released, up to and including *Spectre*?

372. True or false: *SeaFire* is a James Bond novel written by Ian Fleming?

373. What is the first film in which Bond uses a car's ejector seat?

374. Which *Desperate Housewives* actress plays Paris Carver?

375. In what year was the non-Eon version of *Casino Royale* released?

376. Which Bond starred in *On Her Majesty's Secret Service*?

377. How many Bond films have won Academy Awards as of the end of 2020?

378. Which villain is killed by being inflated before floating towards the ceiling and popping?

379. In *Octopussy*, which car does Bond steal while its owner is talking on a payphone?

380. What does SPECTRE stand for?

Turn to page 91 for the answers

381. How do Bond and the other agents reach the North Korean shore at the start of the film?

382. What injury does Zao incur following a C4 explosion?

383. Who plays Jinx?

384. How does Gustav Graves arrive at the ceremony for his knighthood?

385. What sport does Graves notably practice?

386. What is the name of Graves' satellite?

387. How does Zao die?

388. Who kills Miranda Frost?

389. How do Jinx and Bond escape from the plane?

390. Which book does Graves quote when he reunites with his father?

Turn to page 92 for the answers

QUOTES - PART 2

In which Bond film will you hear the following lines?

391. I like to do some things the old-fashioned way.

392. Why is it that people who can't take advice always insist on giving it?

393. Shocking. Positively shocking!

394. You always were a cunning linguist, James.

395. I'm afraid you've caught me with more than my hands up!

396. They're heading for the hills...

397. Any man who drinks Dom Perignon '52 can't be all bad.

398. Bond is of a rare breed, soon to be extinct.

399. Sir Godfrey, on a mission I am expected to sacrifice myself.

400. As you can see, I am about to inaugurate a little war.

Turn to page 93 for the answers

401. How many kills does Bond have to make in order to become a 00 agent?

402. In which embassy does the bomb-maker attempt to take refuge when being chased by Bond?

403. What does Alex Dimitrios wager during his poker game with Bond?

404. To whom is Bond speaking when he says "Oh I'm sorry, that last hand, it nearly killed me"?

405. What type of poker hand does Bond win the game with?

406. Who kills Le Chiffre?

407. What does Bond decide to call the cocktail that he orders?

408. In which country is Casino Royale located?

409. After Bond loses his money, who offers to buy him back into the game?

410. Where does Bond put the explosive device after he removes it from the truck?

Turn to page 94 for the answers

411. Name two films in which throwing knives are used

412. Which villain attacks Bond with dagger shoes?

413. In which film does 007 kill Electra King?

414. True or false: a stuntman was paid a bonus to actually jump into a shark-infested pool during the filming of *Thunderball*?

415. What is Bond's military rank?

416. How many times has James Bond been married?

417. Blofeld appears in 2015's *Spectre*. But in what movie did we last see his face?

418. Which actress has played Moneypenny the most times as of 2021?

419. Name any two actors to have played Q in the Eon franchise.

420. True or false: Shirley Bassey has sung the most James Bond theme songs?

Turn to page 95 for the answers

421. Which Italian city does Bond drive to at the start of the film?

422. What event is taking place as Bond and M are questioning Mr. White?

423. What does Bond collect from the hotel reception in Haiti?

424. What does Dominic Greene ask for as part of his deal with General Medrano?

425. Name the Opera that Bond attends in Austria.

426. What position does Guy Haines hold?

427. Whose body does Bond throw into a dumpster?

428. How does Fields die?

429. With which Government official does M have a meeting?

430. At the charity event, which letter is pinned on Greene's lapel?

Turn to page 96 for the answers

A WHOLE NEW LOW

Here are the ten lowest grossing Bond movies... but not in the correct order. Can you sort them, starting with the lowest?

431. *Live and Let Die*

432. *The Man with the Golden Gun*

433. *From Russia with Love*

434. *A View to a Kill*

435. *Goldfinger*

436. *Licence to Kill*

437. *You Only Live Twice*

438. *The Spy Who Loved Me*

439. *On Her Majesty's Secret Service*

440. *Diamonds Are Forever*

Turn to page 97 for the answers

441. What is Bond attempting to retrieve for MI6 at the start of the film?

442. True or false: Bond waits a full year before returning to MI6?

443. Who stars as the main antagonist, Raoul Silva?

444. How did M supposedly betray Silva?

445. What is Raoul Silva's real name?

446. Which regular Bond cast member's appearance in this film is their last for the franchise?

447. With whom is M when Silva pursues her to the old chapel?

448. How does Bond kill Silva?

449. Where is Bond when he is fighting Silva's last henchman at the end of the film?

450. Filming on *Skyfall* was temporarily halted in 2010, but why?

Turn to page 98 for the answers

451. Which director took the helm for the most Bond films?

452. Which was the first Bond film not to take its title from an Ian Fleming novel?

453. Which character does Charles Gray play in *You Only Live Twice*?

454. What is the first car we see Bond drive in *Dr. No?*

455. Who played Jimmy Bond – an American version of 007 – in an American TV production of *Casino Royale* in 1954?

456. Christopher Lee played a particularly memorable villain in The Man with the Golden Gun. But what relation was he to Ian Fleming?

457. Which 00 agent is murdered in *Octopussy?*

458. How many Academy Awards was *The Spy Who Loved Me* nominated for?

459. Which two Bond films feature Robbie Coltrane?

460. What is the name of Madonna's character in *Die Another Day*?

Turn to page 99 for the answers

461. In *Moonraker*, what is the name of the first of Drax's henchmen to be killed?

462. What shape of spectacles does Locque wear in *For Your Eyes Only*?

463. In *Octopussy*, what is the name of Prince Khan's huge manservant?

464. In which film do we meet Bambi and Thumper?

465. In *The Living Daylights* how does Necros die?

466. Which actor, later to appear in *The Usual Suspects*, plays a henchman in *License To Kill*?

467. When Nick Nack interrupts Bond and Goodnight's lovemaking, how is he dealt with?

468. Who is Elliot Carver's right-hand man?

469. Maria Grazia Cucinotta plays which assassin in *The World Is Not Enough*?

470. In *Die Another Day*, Will Yun Lee plays a character named Colonel Moon. But which 007 author has written a Bond novel called *Colonel Sun*?

Turn to page 100 for the answers

SPECTRE

471. The *Day of the Dead* festival is celebrated in many different countries. But which one do we see in the opening of *Spectre?*

472. A highly respected musician played trumpet on the soundtrack of *Dr. No*, then played on every film until his death in 2013. This made *Spectre* the first Bond film that doesn't feature his talent. What is his name?

473. M16 is determined to keep track of Bond's movements, so they put a supposedly foolproof tracker on him. What form does the tracker take?

474. According to Q, the car that Bond left at the bottom of the river was a prototype, worth how much?

475. Sam Smith sang the theme tune for this film, but with whom did he write it?

476. Bond tracks down an old enemy from whom he obtains some critical information. But who is he?

477. Complete the following quote: "You're a kite..."

478. While following a clue, Bond needs Madeline's help to find something... but what?

479. How does Bond escape from the chair he is strapped to whilst being tortured by Blofeld?

480. At the end of the film what does Bond say to Blofeld when he has him at his mercy?

Turn to page 101 for the answers

HARD ANAGRAMS - VILLAINS & HENCHMEN

Here are some more anagrams of henchmen and villains from the Bond films, but a little harder this time. Can you unscramble each of these?

481. Tenfold Brass Revolt

482. Careful Groin Dig

483. Acorns Facing Maracas

484. Anal Yet Clever

485. Astral Tortoise Skit

486. Lovelorn Rage

487. Fresh Bronze Aura

488. Incredible Them

489. End Ambrosia

490. Neon Germicide

Turn to page 102 for the answers

LYRICS - HARD

And finally some more lyrics for you to sing. What follows these lines?

491. Please don't bet that…

492. His eye may be on you or me. Who…

493. Oh what a trill…

494. Just like the Moonraker goes…

495. The passions that collide in me…

496. I know when to talk and…

497. What did it matter to ya? When…

498. Another girl with her finger on…

499. Hundred thousand people

500. A thousand miles and poles apart, where…

Turn to page 103 for the answers

THE ANSWERS

DR. NO

1. He falls into boiling water

2. The CIA

3. Crab Key

4. Seashells

5. They were radioactive

6. Ursula Andress

7. He is missing both his hands

8. A tarantula

9. *The Daily Gleaner*

10. A Walther PPK

11. Laser beam

12. Crocodiles

13. Funhouse

14. Cremation

15. Dripping poison from a thread

16. Drowning in a lake

17. Chakra torture

18. Teeth

19. Cardiac arrest from poison

20. With her thighs

FROM RUSSIA WITH LOVE

21. Chess

22. A Cipher machine

23. No. 3

24. From Russia With Love

25. A periscope

26. A briefcase with concealed weapons

27. Is your clock correct?

28. Captain Nash

29. The film of himself and Tatiana together

30. Using the hidden knife in the suitcase

FILM YEARS - PART 1

31. 1962

32. 2015

33. 1973

34. 1981

35. 1995

36. 1965

37. 1999

38. 2002

39. 1971

40. 1979

41. 5,000

42. An Aston Martin DB5

43. The passenger seat ejects

44. Jill Masterson spies on his opponent

45. By switching Goldfinger's Golf ball

46. Pussy Galore

47. Geneva in Switzerland

48. Delta 9

49. AU1

50. Being sucked out of a plane's window

GADGETS & GUNS

51. A garroting wire

52. A seagull snorkel

53. An imitation fingerprint

54. His x-ray glasses

55. A lipstick bomb

56. An imitation nipple

57. His ski pole

58. An underwater breather

59. A wrist dart gun

60. A cigarette lighter grenade

61. By using a jetpack

62. NATO

63. Two nuclear bombs

64. An octopus

65. Inside a book

66. The *Disco Valente*

67. With a harpoon

68. Red

69. Clay pigeon shooting

70. Nine

THEME TUNES - PART 1

71. Sheryl Crow

72. Madonna

73. Matt Monro

74. Tina Turner

75. Duran Duran

76. Gladys Knight

77. Nancy Sinatra

78. A-ha

79. Adele

80. Tom Jones

81. It is captured inside another spacecraft

82. Roald Dahl

83. *I Love You*

84. A hitman stabs him in the back

85. Tiger

86. Bon appetite

87. She is poisoned (by mistake, as she is not the target)

88. He sees Bond attempting to enter the space craft carrying his air conditioner

89. Little Nellie

90. It is lifted up by the surfacing of a British submarine

91. Professor Dent

92. By punching him with a knuckle duster

93. He is electrocuted

94. Fiona Volpe

95. 11

96. Irma Bunt

97. Kidd is set on fire and Wint is blown up

98. One of his arms

99. 3'11"

100. Richard Kiel

101. Baccarat

102. Blofeld's location

103. This never happened to the other fella

104. Bullfighting

105. Curling

106. A lady's room number

107. The Angels of Death

108. A kilt

109. Bern in Switzerland

110. The World Is Not Enough

QUOTES - PART 1

111. *Thunderball*

112. *The World Is Not Enough*

113. *Dr. No*

114. *Die Another Day*

115. *Goldfinger*

116. *The Man with the Golden Gun*

117. *Diamonds Are Forever*

118. *Skyfall*

119. *For Your Eyes Only*

120. *Goldeneye*

121. He is thrown into a vat of mud

122. With a scorpion

123. A hovercraft

124. South Africa

125. By comparing fingerprints on a glass slide

126. Craps

127. A moon buggy

128. With a fire extinguisher

129. Shady Tree and His Acorns

130. Felix Leiter

131. Max Zorin

132. Le Chiffre

133. Mr. White

134. Hugo Drax

135. Victor Zokas

136. Raoul Silva

137. Xenia Onatopp

138. Dr. Kananga

139. Elliot Carver

140. Pussy Galore

141. Three

142. It acts as a hyper magnet

143. San Monique

144. Fillet of Soul

145. The fool

146. He crushes it with his metal hand

147. Mr. Big

148. A double-decker bus

149. A hat with a feather in it

150. With a lit cigar and deodorant canister

FILM YEARS - PART 2

151. *Licence to Kill*

152. *On Her Majesty's Secret Service*

153. *Octopussy*

154. *A View to a Kill*

155. *The Spy Who Loved Me*

156. *The Man with the Golden Gun*

157. *Goldfinger*

158. *Quantum of Solace*

159. *The Living Daylights*

160. *Tomorrow Never Dies*

161. Christopher Lee

162. In the mouth of a crow

163. 002

164. His number, 007

165. $1 million

166. The Bottom's Up Club

167. RMS Queen Elizabeth

168. He has a supernumerary (third) nipple

169. Lazar

170. In her belly button

BOND GIRLS

171. Ursula Andress

172. Honor Blackman

173. Diana Rigg

174. Jill St. John

175. Halle Berry

176. Jane Seymour

177. Britt Ekland

178. Maud Adams

179. Gemma Arterton

180. Grace Jones

181. Agent XXX

182. The Union Flag

183. Metal teeth

184. A cigarette with gas in it

185. A microfilm

186. A tea tray

187. A Lotus Esprit

188. A marine biologist

189. Sardinia

190. A cigarette lighter

A GROSS AMOUNT OF MONEY

Here is the correct order, from highest grossing to lowest (of the top ten)…

191. *Skyfall* – $304,360,277

192. *Spectre* – $200,074,609

193. *Quantum of Solace* – $168,368,427

194. *Casino Royale* – $167,445,960

195. *Die Another Day* – $160,942,139

196. *The World Is Not Enough* – $126,943,684

197. *Tomorrow Never Dies* – $125,304,276

198. *Goldeneye* – $106,429,941

199. *Moonraker* – $70,308,099

200. *Octopussy* – $67,893,619

201. Jaws

202. A watch that fires darts

203. Beneath a clock

204. She is mauled to death by hunting dogs

205. Glass

206. The CIA

207. Jaws bites through it

208. Medical personnel

209. A flamethrower

210. A piano

THE NAME'S BOND...

211. Roger Moore

212. Sean Connery

213. Timothy Dalton

214. Pierce Brosnan

215. *The Man With the Golden Gun*

216. Dr. No

217. A-ha

218. Martini, shaken not stirred

219. *On Her Majesty's Secret Service*

220. David Niven

FOR YOUR EYES ONLY

221. Mrs Teresa Bond

222. Blofeld

223. A delicatessen in stainless steel

224. Automatic Targeting and Attack Communicator

225. A naval mine

226. Tofana, 10 am

227. The Dove

228. A white Dove pin

229. She is run over by a beach buggy

230. As ice hockey players

231. …disguise what you fear.

232. …break any heart without regret.

233. …stroke it and undress it.

234. …you know my name.

235. …somehow you found me.

236. …from the shadows as a child.

237. …one life for yourself and one for your dreams.

238. …goodbye to you.

239. …analyse this.

240. …feel the chill.

OCTOPUSSY

241. A fake moustache

242. A fold-up airplane

243. 009

244. *The Property of a Lady*

245. Backgammon

246. With a tracker in his watch

247. Octopussy's Circus

248. Inside a US Air Force Base

249. It has no tyres and thus drives along the track

250. A tennis racket

251. The Golden Gun

252. There are nuclear warheads at the scene of the operation

253. False

254. Seven, including David Niven for the non-Eon version of *Casino Royale*

255. Shirley Bassey, Dionne Warwick or Johnny Cash

256. Five – note that although *Spectre* hadn't been released, it had been filmed

257. Sean Bean

258. Seven, including the non-Eon film *Never Say Never Again*

259. False. It stalled at number two in the UK and only reached number eight in the USA

260. Christmas Jones

261. Heart shaped

262. Christopher Walken

263. Pegasus

264. The Eiffel Tower

265. In the lamp next to his bed

266. At the car wash

267. By setting the elevator on fire

268. Silicon Valley

269. May Day

270. The Golden Gate Bridge

271. Octopussy

272. Live and Let Die

273. Goldfinger

274. A View to a Kill

275. Casino Royale

276. Moonraker

277. Thunderball

278. GoldenEye

279. Licence to Kill

280. Spectre

281. Gibraltar

282. Through the Trans-Siberian Pipeline

283. A ghetto blaster

284. Death to Spies

285. A milkman

286. Rule, Britannia!

287. John Rhys-Davis

288. Jerzy Bondov

289. Kara Milovy's cello case

290. An organ transplant container

NEVER SAY NEVER

291. *Moonraker*

292. Two

293. Vodka Martini, shaken not stirred

294. Most connoisseurs would ask for theirs to be stirred, not shaken

295. Ernst Stavro Blofeld

296. Georgian

297. She can read the future from tarot cards

298. Omega

299. *Quantum of Solace*

300. Four – Bernard Lee, Robert Brown, Judi Dench and Ralph Fiennes

LICENSE TO KILL

301. By connecting his plane to the coast guard's helicopter

302. By parachute

303. By feeding him to a shark

304. A manta ray

305. Sharkey

306. He uses a ramp to pull the tanker to one side

307. Gasoline

308. An iguana

309. The Republic of Isthmus

310. A tube of toothpaste

THEME TUNES - PART 2

311. *We Have All the Time in the World*

312. *All Time High*

313. *For Your Eyes Only*

314. *Writing's on the Wall*

315. *You Know My Name*

316. *The Man with the Golden Gun*

317. *Kingston Calypso*

318. *Live and Let Die*

319. *Nobody Does It Better*

320. *Another Way to Die*

321. By bungee jumping from the top of a dam

322. Sean Bean

323. *The Manticore*

324. Eurocopter Tiger

325. An electromagnetic pulse will be fired

326. Janus

327. Beneath a lake

328. *Stand by Your Man*

329. A bag inflates and traps him against the glass

330. Three minutes

331. *Melina Havelock*

332. *My Word Is My Bond*

333. *A View to a Kill*

334. Lazar

335. An AMC Hornet X

336. True – even though it was only 1974!

337. Just one

338. A fear of guns

339. 2003

340. True

341. An American GPS Encoder

342. Back seat driver!

343. Jonathan Pryce

344. British Sailors Murdered

345. Danish

346. A car-hire salesman

347. Dr Kaufman

348. A giant banner

349. *Tomorrow*

350. With his mobile phone

351. The Living Daylights

352. Never Say Never Again

353. For Your Eyes Only

354. You Only Live Twice

355. Diamonds Are Forever

356. The World Is Not Enough

357. Tomorrow Never Dies

358. From Russia with Love

359. Die Another Day

360. The Spy Who Loved Me

361. In his spectacles

362. Oh Moneypenny, the story of our relationship: close, but no cigar!

363. The Millennium Dome

364. Five million dollars

365. 009

366. Feel pain

367. X-ray spectacles

368. False – she's a doctor of nuclear physics

369. A basic high-card draw

370. He has a jacket which contains a rapidly-inflating sphere

371. Twenty-four (*No Time to Die* had not actually been released at the time of writing)

372. False – it *is* a Bond novel but was written by John Gardner

373. *Goldfinger*

374. Teri Hatcher

375. 1967

376. George Lazenby

377. Four – *Goldfinger* (Best Sound Effects), *Thunderball* (Best Special Visual Effects), *Skyfall* (Best Original Song and Best Sound Editing) and *Spectre* (Best Original Song)

378. Dr. Kananga / Mr. Big

379. Alfa Romeo GTV6

380. Special Executive for Counter-intelligence, Terrorism, Revenge and Extortion

381. By surfing

382. One half of his face is impaled with diamonds

383. Halle Berry

384. He parachutes into Buckingham Palace

385. Fencing

386. Icarus

387. He is impaled underneath a chandelier

388. Jinx

389. They fall from the plane whilst actually inside a helicopter

390. *The Art of War*

QUOTES - PART 2

391. *Skyfall*

392. *Casino Royale*

393. *Goldfinger*

394. *Tomorrow Never Dies*

395. *Diamonds Are Forever*

396. *Live and Let Die*

397. *The Spy Who Loved Me*

398. *Octopussy*

399. *A View to a Kill*

400. *You Only Live Twice*

CASINO ROYALE

401. Two

402. The embassy of Nambutu

403. His Aston Martin DB5

404. Le Chiffre

405. A straight flush

406. Mr. White

407. A Vesper

408. Montenegro

409. Felix Leiter

410. On Carlos's belt buckle

411. Any of *Moonraker, For Your Eyes Only, Octopussy, The World Is Not Enough* and *Skyfall*

412. Rosa Klebb

413. *The World is Not Enough*

414. True, amazingly!

415. Commander

416. Just the once

417. *Diamonds Are Forever.* Although Bond encounters him in the pre-credits of *For Your Eyes Only*, he is not referred to by name and we never actually see his face!

418. Lois Maxwell

419. Any of Peter Burton (Who appeared in *Dr. No*, though he is not referred to as Q in the film itself), Desmond Llewelyn, John Cleese and Ben Whishaw

420. True

421. Siena

422. A horse race

423. A briefcase

424. A piece of land in the Bolivian desert

425. *Tosca*

426. Special Advisor to the Prime Minister

427. René Mathis

428. He is drowned in oil

429. The Home Secretary

430. Q

A WHOLE NEW LOW

431. *The Man with the Golden Gun* – $20,972,000

432. *On Her Majesty's Secret Service* – $22,774,493

433. *From Russia with Love* – $24,796,765

434. *Licence to Kill* – $34,667,015

435. *Live and Let Die* – $35,377,836

436. *You Only Live Twice* – $43,084,787

437. *Diamonds Are Forever* – $43,819,547

438. *The Spy Who Loved Me* – $46,838,673

439. *A View to a Kill* – $50,327,960

440. *Goldfinger* – $51,081,062

441. A hard drive containing the names of NATO agents embedded in terrorist organisations

442. False – it is closer to three months

443. Javier Bardem

444. She sent him into the field when he wasn't ready; he was traded to the enemy

445. Tiago Rodriguez

446. Dame Judi Dench

447. Kincade, the gamekeeper

448. He throws a knife into his back

449. In a lake

450. The film's producer – MGM – was suffering from financial troubles

PISTOLS AT DAWN

451. John Glen (with eight films)

452. *License to Kill*

453. Henderson

454. A Sunbeam Alpine

455. Barry Nelson

456. They were cousins

457. 009

458. Three: Best Art Direction, Best Original Score and Best Original Song

459. *GoldenEye* and *The World is Not Enough*

460. Verity

461. Chang

462. Octagonal

463. Gobinda

464. *Diamonds Are Forever*

465. He falls from an airplane

466. Benico Del Toro

467. Bond locks him in a suitcase

468. Stamper

469. Cigar Girl

470. Robert Markham

471. Mexico

472. Derek Watkins

473. Microchips in his blood

474. Three million pounds

475. Jimmy Napes

476. Mr. White

477. "…dancing in a hurricane, Mr. Bond"

478. L'Americain

479. With his exploding watch

480. I've got something better to do

HARD ANAGRAMS - VILLAINS & HENCHMEN

481. Ernst Stavro Blofeld

482. Auric Goldfinger

483. Francisco Scaramanga

484. Alec Trevelyan

485. Aristotle Kristatos

486. General Orlov

487. Franz Oberhauser

488. Three Blind Mice

489. Baron Samedi

490. Dominic Greene

LYRICS - HARD

491. …you'll ever escape me.

492. …will he bang? We shall see!

493. …vacillations good lord.

494. …in search of his dream of gold.

495. …the wild abandoned side of me.

496. …I know when to touch.

497. …you got a job to do, you got to do it well.

498. …the world singing to ya what you wanna hear.

499. …I'm the one they blame.

500. …worlds collide and days are dark.

Chris McAuley
Jack Goldstein

101 AMAZING FACTS ABOUT

JAMES
BOND

UNOFFICIAL & UNAUTHORISED